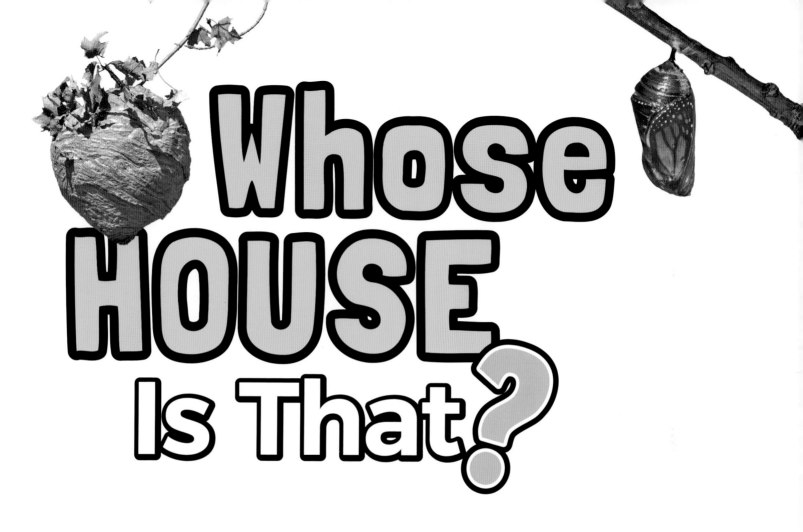

Whose HOUSE Is That?

by **Stan Tekiela**

Adventure Publications
Cambridge, Minnesota

Dedication

To Abby, with all my love.

Front Cover: (wasp nest) by Nancy Bauer/shutterstock.com; (monarch chrysalis) by Leena Robinson/shutterstock.com; (robin nest) by Devin Koob/shutterstock.com; (beaver lodge) by Stan Tekiela; (burrow and background) by Piotr Szpakowski/shutterstock.com; (prairie dog head) by Stan Tekiela

Back Cover: (bald eagle nest) by Stan Tekiela

All photos by Stan Tekiela except pg. 37 by Chriscunningham/shutterstock.com; pg. 38 by Massimo Todaro/shutterstock.com; pg. 39 by MattiaATH/shutterstock.com; pg. 41 "Baby Bunny Nest" (adjusted) by Flickr user Lisa Zins; pg. 46 by Ant Cooper/shutterstock.com

Cover and book design by Jonathan Norberg

10 9 8 7 6 5 4 3 2 1

Whose House Is That?
Copyright © 2021 by Stan Tekiela
Published by Adventure Publications
An imprint of AdventureKEEN
310 Garfield Street South
Cambridge, Minnesota 55008
(800) 678-7006
www.adventurepublications.net
Printed in China
ISBN 978-1-64755-074-5

This home is perched
up in a tree, but it's almost
as large as your bedroom!

It's made of sticks
and branches. Our national
symbol lives there.

Whose house is that?

It's a Bald Eagle!

The **Bald Eagle** is the national symbol of the United States. The eagle uses its nest over and over for many years, adding new sticks to it each year. Some nests get so large that they can be ten feet tall and weigh a thousand pounds. That is about the same weight as a horse. An eagle nest is called an aerie (say it, *air*-ee).

Small and round, this home
is constructed of mud and grass.
It is the perfect size
for one mommy and her
eggs. You might even have
one in your own yard.

Whose house is that?

It's an American Robin!

The **American Robin** is a common bird found almost everywhere in North America, from your backyard to the tops of the highest mountains. Both parents build a nest for the eggs. This house takes just three to four days to complete. Mothers lay three to five bright blue eggs in the nest, and soon there are baby robins!

Larger than a football, this home hangs in a tree, or may even be under your deck or attached to your house. This home holds hundreds, maybe thousands, of individuals inside.

Whose house is that?

It's a Bald-faced Hornet!

The **Bald-faced Hornet** doesn't have a bald face. It also actually isn't a hornet. It's a wasp with a white face. Its dark eyes make it look bald. It builds its home, called a nest, by mixing tiny pieces of chewed-up tree wood with its saliva (spit). Because the nest looks like it's made of paper, these wasps are often mistakenly called Paper Wasps.

Something amazing happens inside this shiny, bright green house. One kind of critter goes in and a completely different one comes out. It's like magic.

Whose house is that?

It's a Monarch Butterfly!

When the Monarch caterpillar reaches full size, it does something amazing. Its back splits open and its outer skin falls off, leaving behind a hanging green bag, called a chrysalis (say it, *criss-uh-lis*). This chrysalis is kind of like a home. Inside the green bag, the caterpillar changes into the black-and-orange **Monarch Butterfly**.

This house can be as big as your family's car. It is made of large branches and tree trunks. This home is usually near water.

Whose house is that?

It's an American Beaver!

The **American Beaver** is an expert craftsman. It builds a large home, called a lodge, with sticks and branches. The lodge has an underwater entrance, but inside it is dry and warm. The entire family lives inside. They eat the soft and juicy bark from tree branches. When they are done eating all the bark, they use the leftovers to build their lodge and a dam.

This home is usually underground. The residents live there for up to six months without leaving. These homes are warm and dry compared to the winter weather outside.

Whose house is that?

It's a **Black Bear!**

The **American Black Bear** often makes its house under a fallen tree, or it will dig a hole in the ground. This kind of home is called a den. Bears only use their dens during winter. Mothers give birth to their babies while in the den. Some dens are small and cozy while others are large and comfortable.

This home is strung between tall grasses or twigs and tree branches. This net-like home is also very sticky.

Whose house is that?

It's a Garden Spider!

The **Yellow Garden Spider**, also called the Argiope Spider, weaves a round web, called an orb, that can be up to two feet wide. At the center of the web is a dense zigzag pattern of spider silk. Some scientists think this special part of the web attracts flying insects, which are then caught in it.

This home looks more like a mound of dirt than a comfortable place to live. The mound also serves as a lookout for the critters who live in this home.

Whose house is that?

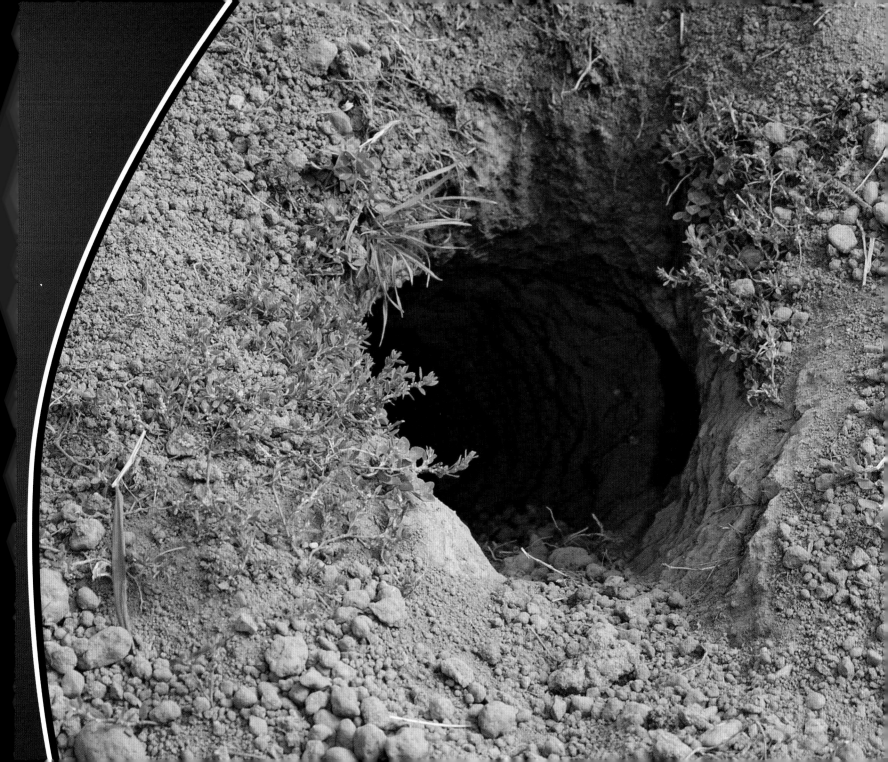

It's a Prairie Dog!

The **Black-tailed Prairie Dog** digs a network of underground tunnels and chambers, called a burrow. It is large enough for its entire family to live in. The burrow has separate chambers for storing food, sleeping and playing. It's like a huge home with many rooms. There is even a chamber for their bathroom.

This home is wet and sandy and shaped like a shallow dish.

Whose house is that?

It's a Sunfish!

The **Sunfish** is a common fish that is found in many lakes and rivers. A sunfish makes a shallow depression, called a bed, just offshore by wiggling its tail and pushing out all plants and exposing the gravel bottom. That is where it lays its eggs and the babies hatch.

This home is warm, dry, soft and cozy. The floor, walls and even the roof are made of fluffy fur.

Whose house is that?

It's a Cottontail Rabbit!

A female **Cottontail Rabbit** digs a shallow dip in the ground. Next, she makes it comfortable by lining it with some of her own fur. This cozy home is called a burrow. If several females make their homes close together, the group of burrows is called a warren. Sometimes there are three or four brothers and sisters born together in these homes.

This home may be tiny
when compared to your home.
It is made up of many underground
tunnels and chambers.
The home's entrance is a small hill.

Whose house is that?

It's a Common Ant!

A family of **Ants** is called a colony. The ants dig a large network of tunnels underground. When they bring some of the dirt or sand to the earth's surface they make a mound called an anthill. All the tunnels together are called a nest, and this is where the ants all live.

It's your turn!

Now it's time for you to find the animal houses near you. Go on a scavenger hunt in a green space, a park or your backyard, and see how many animal houses you can find. Once you start looking, you'll likely find all sorts of them. How many can you find?

Safety Note: Don't get too close to an animal house or put your hands in or near one, as you don't want to surprise any inhabitants! Always have an adult help you look, keep your distance, and wear gloves.

HERE ARE SOME TYPES OF ANIMAL HOUSES TO LOOK FOR

- ☐ Bird houses or nests
- ☐ Squirrel drays (leaf nests in trees)
- ☐ Anthills
- ☐ Spiderwebs
- ☐ Beehives (from a distance)
- ☐ Insect tunnels underneath tree bark
- ☐ Gopher tunnels
- ☐ Molehills
- ☐ Hollow logs
- ☐ Cavities in a tree